DANCING ON THE BRINK OF THE WORLD
Selected Poems of Point L

D0763741

June 22, 2003

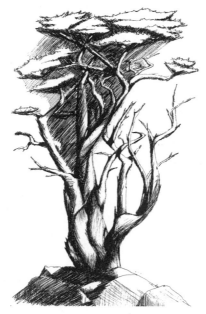

DANCING
ON THE BRINK
OF THE WORLD
Selected Poems of Point Lobos

edited by
DEBORAH STREETER

drawings by
SALLY SMITH

POINT LOBOS NATURAL HISTORY ASSOCIATION
Point Lobos State Reserve, Route 1, Box 62, Carmel, CA 93923

(paperback) 9 8 7 6 5 4 3 2 1

DANCING ON THE BRINK OF THE WORLD
Selected Poems of Point Lobos
Book copyright © 2003 Point Lobos Natural History Association
Selection, Introduction and Notes on Contributors copyright © 2003
        by Deborah Streeter.
Art copyright © 2003 by Sally Smith.

Library of Congress Catalogue Card No. 2003092207

ISBN 0-9740950-0-1

Printed on recycled paper with soy ink.

Table of Contents

Introduction

Point Lobos State Reserve is more than just a promontory of rocks and trees and ocean and animals. Here, profound power and mystery and soul permeate the landscape. Point Lobos sings of time and beauty and loss, of rough and gentle, depth and bud, bark and blow and silence.

To visit Point Lobos is to become a poet. Each visitor hears, in wave against granite, the language of the soul. Many a visitor tries to respond creatively to the calls of this wild beauty and might. For poets seasoned and novice, the exterior landscape evokes an interior wisdom, wonder, awe.

For longer than recorded history, Point Lobos has inspired poets and artists. The title of this collection of poems, *Dancing on the Brink of the World*, comes from a single fragment of a lost ancient Ohlone Indian song.* I imagine the native people of this area, the Ohlone, finding here not only physical sustenance - - abalone and sage - -, but in this holy place spiritual sustenance too. I can see the Ohlone dancing, thousands of years ago, on this brink.

From Bohemians to Beats to today, poets have found inspiration at Point Lobos. Early in the last century, George Sterling and others held long, drunken picnics at Point Lobos, adding verse after verse to his delightful "Abalone Song." But Sterling also wrote about Point Lobos in the deeply mystical "Altar of the West", inspired perhaps by his love for fellow poet Nora May French, whose ashes he scattered at Point Lobos in 1907.

*Quoted in Malcolm Margolin's The Ohlone Way, Indian Life in the San Francisco-Monterey Bay Area, Heydey Books, Berkeley, 1978, p. 4

Robinson Jeffers looked out at Point Lobos every day from his stone house and stone tower on Carmel Point. Between 1918 and 1924 Jeffers built Tor House and Hawk Tower by hand from the same granite that is the foundation of Point Lobos. His large body of poetry dramatized "this coast crying out for tragedy." Jeffers' popularity and acclaim brought many other poets to the Central Coast.

Indeed, the inspiration for this collection of poetry came from the frequent comment by visitors, "I first heard about Point Lobos from reading Robinson Jeffers. Are there other poems about this special place?"

Curious about this question, I began in 2001 to search for Point Lobos poems. I found many in the newsletters of the Point Lobos Natural History Association and the Docent Association. Both have included poetry for over 20 years. Then I spent hours scouring the collections in the History Rooms of the Carmel and Monterey Public Libraries and talking with local poets. I was surprised and delighted to find poems by such American giants as Eric Barker, Robert Bly and Michael McClure.

But even more delightful was the discovery of so many poems by so-called amateurs. Visiting Point Lobos has emboldened docents, locals, tourists, and school children to attempt the language of the soul. I invite you to read more about each contributor, professional and amateur, in the back of the book.

There were many more poems than I had room for, and for some poems I was unable to locate the poet or acquire permission, especially for many of the school children's poems. I have placed in the Docent Library at Point Lobos a complete collection of all the Point Lobos poems I found. My thanks to Ranger Chuck Bancroft who has encouraged visiting school children to hear and write poems about Point Lobos and has been the unofficial guardian of Point Lobos poems for over 20 years.

Two Central Coast poets deserve special note, and thanks. Ric Masten and Elliot Ruchowitz-Roberts have advised and encouraged me from the start of this project, and done everything from finding poet addresses to proofreading. Ric Masten is this book's fine designer, as well as a contributing poet.

How to organize the presentation of these 55 poems, written from 1905 to 2002, by a wild variety of authors? By subject or place or date? I have chosen to organize the chapters, loosely, by subject. The six different chapters offer poems about rocks, the sea, trees, animals, artists and mystery or spirit. Each chapter's title is a phrase from a poem in that chapter.

But none of these poems are really "about" just one thing, be it cypress or otter or cliff. Each poet had an experience at Point Lobos that evoked an insight, a question, a feeling. Place side by side two poems written about the same thing, for example, about whales (Don Marsh and Eric Barker, pp. 46-47) and compare how the same animal evoked such different poetry. Or two wave poems by Jeanne D'Orge and Ann Muto, pp.22-23. Read the four very different poems explicitly "about" cypress trees, and then imagine how you would write a poem "about" cypress, and what they evoke in you. And what they might stir in you tomorrow.

Sally Smith's pen and ink drawings are included not as illustrations, but as visual poems. She writes of her work: "From the beginning of my stay in California in 1995, Point Lobos has been a place of restoration. Together with another artist wife of a faculty member at the new California State University at Monterey Bay, I would go to paint and to draw the landscape of my new home most like the landscape of my childhood in Maine. With my friend, I discovered the incredible colors of the Pacific, the incidental artistry of the coastal trees and rocks, the antics of the waterborne and land based animals and birds. These drawings were done over a year's time, 2002-2003, generally in the winter-spring, when Point Lobos is at its most quiet. I am honored to have them in this book."

Sally and I offer this book not just as a collection of poems and art by others, but as an invitation for you, the readers, to become poets and artists yourself. We have intentionally left some large blank spaces in the body of the book, and some extra pages at the back. <u>We want you to write and draw in this book!</u> Become a poet and artist yourself, just as many of these works were done by first time creators.

We include also a rough map identifying where some of the poems or drawings "take place." We invite you to go to these spots yourself, and there speak the language of your soul onto these pages or into the wind. Perhaps your creations will fill a Volume Two!

Point Lobos has been called "the grandest meeting of land and sea." It is indeed a brink on the edge of the world. Poetry celebrates meetings, brinks, contrasts, doorsteps between body and soul, public and private, secular and spiritual, beauty and terror. May you enter this special spiritual place with a poet's heart. As you cross over that doorstep and stand on that brink, may your inner poet and artist speak alongside those in this book.

Deborah Streeter, Editor

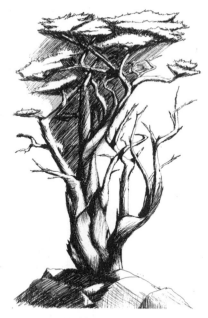

DANCING
ON THE BRINK
OF THE WORLD
Selected Poems of Point Lobos

Chapter One

THE MASSIVE
MYSTICISM OF STONE

SOME ROCKS OFF POINT LOBOS NEAR CHINA COVE

These rocks are poking out into the sea.
What shall we call them?
Sedimentary onions of surprise,
Giant pebbles of sadness,
Advance agents of the watery government that never came
        into power,
Mineral strategians watching for approaching eternity,
Angelic hearts of disappointed stone,
Lamenting that the Mesopotamians never arrived,
Inert lodgers who pay no rent to the ocean,
But live on the nourishing shadows left by gull wings,
Settlers of questions tougher than Hegel ever dreamt of,
Widows of the great whales,
Ringers of a grandfather clock that has stopped,
Teeth of the Gnostic sorrow,
Sentinels at the door of the Archons' kingdom,
Our brothers waiting centuries for God to come.

-Robert Bly, 2002

SAND AND SEA

Sea coming to sand
sand and sea mixing and dancing together
ripples farther out
changing colors — blue and gray
sand holes in the midst of the mix
vegetation under the waves
flowing and changing together
leaving the sand wet and marked
leaving the ocean gray and sand-swirled
washing together: the sand and the sea

-Dustin Katz, 2002

ROCK AND HAWK

Here is a symbol in which
Many high tragic thoughts
Watch their own eyes.

This gray rock, standing tall
On the headland, where the seawind
Lets no tree grow,

Earthquake-proved, and signatured
By ages of storms: on its peak
A falcon has perched.

I think, here is your emblem
To hang in the future sky;
Not the cross, not the hive,

But this; bright power, dark peace;
Fierce consciousness joined with final
Disinterestedness;

Life with calm death; the falcon's
Realist eyes and act
Married to the massive

Mysticism of stone,
Which failure cannot cast down
Nor success make proud.

-Robinson Jeffers, 1939

POINT LOBOS*

The surf song sings in the ringing woods
Where the great pine flowers grow,
And lying on your back you see them
Dancing to and fro;
And the haloed light through the branches bright
Makes a silver web in the lover's sight
Whose heart from the damp earth reaches out
To the plea in the wind from the sea.

Where the gull-knolled rocks cock their ears and sigh
To the waves that breach in the cove,
Fly my dancing feet with a wood fawn's beat
With the windblown rhyme of the clouds that go
In a sunlight swirl with a world's end whirl
Toward the lips of the wolf which curl
Where the pine and the cypress wave in the wind;
Where the whales rise and blow for air.
Where the divers dive in the deep green sea
While the wildcat waits in its lair.

Oh, Whaler's Cove and Cypress Point!
Oh, forest yet unmarred!
Where the diamonds made of light all blaze
On the rolling, wave-rocked sward;
A meadow full of kelp and shells
Curved in the sandy cove
Round the great humped rocks
Where the growing flocks
Of pelicans betroth
On the rock lean shanks
Of the wolf's steep flanks,
On the sharp points of his spine,
This beast who rests half in Neptune's world,
And the other half in mine.

-Josh Jossi, 1986

Los lobos = the wolves

in the mortar
of the living rock

       touched

          pounded

in the flesh cove
marrow of the dream

       whispered

          revealed

by the unspanned
canyon of the sea

       brine scented

          and hallowed

thrown in white foam
with all the seal spring

       so known and

          swallowed

-John Dotson, 1989

HUSH!

Hush!
If you lie close to a rock in the silence of the sun
you hear.
You will not hear with the outer ear
but you will hear
thunder.
It will sound through the rock and through your body.
You will tremble as the rock trembles
at so terrible a sound.
To the end of time you shall never know
if it was the heart of the rock or your heart
or the sea...

-Jeanne D'Orge, 1928

5 THOUGHTS OF POINT LOBOS

Shreds of mist
lay on the coast,
and time has stopped.
The first morning,
The first spring

The gull with one eye
watches us eating
here by the sea

This endless sea,
This brilliant sun,
This special shore,
This morning washed of yesterday

Winter sagebrush camphor like
has lost its springtime freshness

Anywhere,
at anytime,
the heart sits
on a rock above the sea

-Ed Huenerfauth, 1999

Chapter Two

SHIMMERED WITH SILVER,
SURGE ON SWEEPING SURGE

CONTINENT'S END

At the equinox when the earth was veiled in a late rain,
    wreathed with wet poppies, waiting spring,
The ocean swelled for a far storm and beat its boundary, the
    ground-swell shook the beds of granite.

I gazing at the boundaries of granite and spray, the established
    sea-marks, felt behind me
Mountain and plain, the immense breadth of the continent,
    before me the mass and doubled stretch of water.

I said: You yoke the Aleutian seal-rocks with the lava and coral
    sowings that flower the south,
Over your flood the life that sought the sunrise faces ours that
    has followed the evening star.

The long migrations meet across you and it is nothing to you,
    you have forgotten us, mother.
You were much younger when we crawled out of the womb and
    lay in the sun's eye on the tideline.

It was long and long ago; we have grown proud since then and
    you have grown bitter; life retains
Your mobile soft unquiet strength; and envies hardness, the
    insolent quietness of stone.

The tides are in our veins, we still mirror the stars, life is your
    child, but there is in me
Older and harder than life and more impartial, the eye that
    watched before there was an ocean.

That watched you fill your beds out of the condensation of thin
    vapor and watched you change them,
That saw you soft and violent wear your boundaries down, eat
    rock, shift places with the continents.

Mother, though my song's measure is like your surf-beat's
        ancient rhythm I never learned it of you.
Before there was any water there were tides of fire, both our
        tones flow from the older fountain.

-Robinson Jeffers, 1937

I HEAR IT FAR AWAY AND DOWN

I hear it far away and down
down under the sea.
The sound rushes up from the caves beneath the cliff
louder when a wave breaks;
but it is not the sound of a broken wave
(there are chariot wheels in that and horses' hoofs
and rough sailor voices shouting)
It is not the wind—yet it is music—
it is an orchestra—a full orchestra
playing a mad waltz time and a madder jig time
to a dizzy wild tune that will never stop,
never to the end of the world.

I do not know who plays
far away and down
down under the sea;
but I know who they are that dance there—
who come shouting in chariots—shouting on horseback.
I know they are dead sailors with their bright sea brides
all the dead sailors
none missing—not one since the first ship drowned—
and could I find another way to go there
I would be dancing too.

-Jeanne D'Orge, 1928

DELUGE
West of Granite Point

over the everlasting
body of the Pacific

the serpent tide
uncoils in iridescent

deluge flooding
this secluded cove

and resides here still

quietly

aquamarine

     *

tongues resonate
with brine and woodmint

the light has changed

a solemnity of three
pelicans

cruise

     *

shadowclouds
of blackbirds swell

and break evenly
flash white and

16

turn back across
a thousand petaled

moon

  *

illuminated
in the waves

you bend to
quicken

  *

fingers diverge

like open wings
now leading

to the center of deepest need

  *

where loving lives
living dances

your eyes have lifted

  *

the rest of your life
you are free

                    -John Dotson, 1991

I

I heard old Lobos storming in the night
   Through all the clefts and caverns; and the sound
   Swept from the craggy crests and deeps profound
Up to the stars within the zenith height.
What a mad tumult! Waves with fangs of white
   Gnawed at the rocky bases; bound on bound
   Leaped up the cliff sides to the lofty ground
Where the gaunt cypress trees defied their might.

I heard old Lobos storming, hurling wide
   Its trumpet of defiance to the seas,
   Daring them on, and flinging back their roar;
   Above in calm looked down the Pleiades;
Above, Orion with majestic stride
   Moved on far over that wild line of shore.

II

In the mad midday tempest came a lull;
   The sun flamed out and touched with slanting gold
The white wings of a gull.

The sea that had been gray and stark and cold
   Shimmered with silver, surge on sweeping surge
Radiantly aureoled.
And all the wide horizon seemed to merge
   In dancing hues; a ship with high bright hull
Poised on the gleaming verge.

Calm after storm—a scene how beautiful!
   As on the restless ocean of our life
   Peace after strife;
In the mad midday tempest came a lull.

III

The breakers cream, the breakers comb,
    Where Lobos lifts its massive wall;
It seems to be the haunt and home
    Of an unrest perpetual.

Around the rampart's beetling verge,
    Above the jagged reach of shore,
The great winds sound a vibrant dirge
    Forever and forevermore.

Now low the music dips and dies
    In weird and wailing undertones,
And now it swells and mounts the skies
    As with despairing seamen's moans.

One who from Lobos fronts the seas,
    One who from Lobos harks and hears,
Will have wild haunting memories
    Through the succession of his years.

IV

Who has not looked on Lobos has not seen
Nature in tragic majesty of mien.

Who has not trod on Lobos has not known
The face of Wonder intimately shown.

Who has not stood on Lobos lingeringly
Has never felt the passion of the sea.

Dawn—noon—eve—midnight—the diurnal law;
And upon Lobos an eternal awe!

-Clinton Scollard, 1925

NEW YEAR'S DAY

I carry with me, in my heart,
One who is thirsty for the sea,
I know he watches, far away,
Pacific spray, anointing me.

Point Lobos in the afternoon
Time fashioned cypress, crystal air.
Bright ocean ripples on the rocks,
Exalting in a joyfelt prayer.

I often keep a vigil there,
In foggy sheltered majesty,
Beside a wind-swept sculpted bear
Holding out his hand to me.

-Illia Thompson, 2002

MARCH EQUINOX 1996
(Looking south from Carmel Point)

Point Lobos cuts the sea.
Gray horse waves
Climb the dark rocks,
White manes flying.

-Jean Grace, 1996

FOAM FLOWERS SPRING FROM SPRAY

Foam flowers spring from spray—
bud and bloom and break away
into a million million glittering seeds
all in one moment.
All in one moment they are scattered—
the wave takes them in soft shining hands
scatters and weaves them in and out
into a pattern of delicate silken lace—
lace for a scarf.
There are no words sheer enough to tell of that scarf
or of the floating silver serpent curves it makes
winding about a rock.

Sometimes it stays there a long while—
sometimes the wind whisks it off
and back to the merchant sea.

-Jeanne D'Orge, 1928

THE SLOT

One could say the ocean's angry
When its white spray explodes against the rocks
When it hurls itself with reckless abandon
Crashing here and there

Sometimes gathering itself for a concerted assault
Celebrating in an awesome display
Of power and unpredictability
Sometimes relaxing
And flowing gracefully down the rocks towards shore
Sometimes bursting again
Its spray leaping up, mocking the gods
Laughing as the humans run for cover

There is no denying its power
But is it lashing out in anger
Or frolicking in play

-Ann Muto, 1993

Chapter Three

WHAT DESPERATE FAITH
WRITHES IN THESE TWISTED LIMBS?

CLIFF CYPRESSES

Food from the granite
  Stone for the hungry root -
  Storm for the rugged shoot.
What slow flame
  Struggles to triumph here
  Year upon difficult year?
What desperate faith
  Writhes in these twisted limbs,
  Sings in the wordless hymns?
When the rock splits
  They wrestle with each other,
  Brother contrives with brother
For writhing's sake.
  No peace can smooth or define
  A curve, a delicate line.
Summers burn blue -
  Yet the torture wrought in the seed
  In anguished form is freed
Torture and triumph!
  These for whom pain is duty
  Stand in their desperate beauty.

-Dora Hagemeyer, 1947

CYPRESS TREES AT POINT LOBOS

These forms of flight, of agony, of flame,
Reach their gaunt branches to the sky,
Writhing away from earth in desperate gesture
Silvered with countless storms, silked by the wind,
Whitened by lash and age and the salt spray -
What is their speech for the child of pilgrimage
Who comes to their rock-crashed garden?

This angular despair the heart knows
Elbowing away from grace -
This furious refusal -
Yet they have not escaped love!
Against the oncoming urgence of the ocean
Their intervals are blue with song,
And at their feet
The importunate wild flowers
Pay no attention to their epic sorrow,
But smother their ankles with a million garlands.

-Dora Hagemeyer, 1953

AT POINT LOBOS

Four nuns flap on the beach
and squirrels eat from our hands.
The spindliest pines I've ever seen
grow here - a forest of bird legs.

On the bluffs the cypresses
pose like dancers. We face
the lavender sea, leaning backward.
Slowly, my limbs begin to twist.

A white-crowned sparrow lands
on my thigh. In future years
you might find me on a sea cliff
in wind, stiff, alive.

-Lucille Lang Day, 2002

POINT LOBOS CYPRESSES

It is good to walk along this shore again
And rest beneath the ancient trees.
Change comes slowly here; the herring gulls
That hang above the sea might be the birds
We watched last year from this same place,
Over the heaving kelp, among the tide-rocks.
Through the dark trees, searching all the grove
With sound, beats the huge orchestration of the surf.
For centuries the sea-notes shatter here
Before the titans fall. Their lives are nobler
Than any man's saving Prometheus.
He too, the Rock-Bound, endured such sun
And wind, the mordant fire of salt
Working his creviced wounds, and when
The great shocks shuddered through the cliff
Tensed all his strength, feeling the rock-base
Shaken beneath his feet, the bellowing aurochs
Plunging in the caves.

These giants would knit a pygmy heart
With fortitude for life. I could make gods
Of these, and when full circle came,
Envy their nobler death; ours the dank grave,
The old decaying flesh, the wormy dark.
But see how these grey bones
Are picked clean by the surf,
Consumed in the foam's white fire....

Old trees beautiful and dying,
Centuries dying, be here at the end.
When man's last war has killed the race
And left the planet clean I can see you then -
Old trees beautiful and dying,
Centuries dying on the granite cliffs,
Alone on Lobos, by the smoking sea.

-Eric Barker, 1956

31

VETERAN CYPRESS

Rugged beauty on continent's edge,
your rounded canopy swept by fog
gives little hint of your ultimate fate.
Below, in the canyon, your gnarled roots
cling, oh so firmly, to weathered stone;
and above, your thickened buttress stands
rock-solid, fixing that massive trunk.

Yet, even now, your buttress splits,
and adjacent slopes are strewn with limbs.
Are you aware, old veteran, of your destiny?
But then . . . do any of us know?

-Curt Cureton, 1996

Only the trees tell
Earth will never.
She has ordered the rocks into silence;
She has crammed the mouth of the cliff with flowers;
it can but sigh with honey breath.

Only the trees tell
and not all the trees.
A few know and even these dare not speak the horror
but stand transfixed in flight
forever fleeing - forever bound
forever doomed to turn and twist and writhe
in a strange still torment.
They cannot forget - they dare not speak -
even in death their whitened bones
still writhe
still twist
still turn.

-Jeanne D'Orge, 1928

Chapter Four

WESTWARD
THE WAVE-GLEANERS

ENOUGH WORDS

In the constantly peaking sea,
an otter floats on its back
in blindingly bright reflections.
One gull stands on the crest
of a stony outcropping...watching
photographers on Weston Beach.

A cormorant drifts in the waves.
I want to tell you
how light oscillates
and dances off the water,
but I don't have enough words.
Maybe no one has all the words.
You have to see it.

I want to tell you how surf howls.
You have to hear it.
You have to smell salt drying
in pools of granite and the scent
of two hundred pines standing together
defying the Pacific Ocean.

You have to stroke the curvature
of grain in cypress driftwood,
its gray and silver layers flowing
like a landscape of rivers.
I can't tell you what the rocks
in the distance know, surrounded
as they are with thin mists.

I don't have enough words.
I come again into the tide and the land
like the solitary gull that turns
its head first to the sea,
then to shore,
needing nothing more.

-Laura Bayless, 1997

MY DEAD SEAL

Robert Bly's seal was in Pt. Reyes
My seal in Pt. Lobos — Gibson Beach
Both were dying

He took the time to "see" the whole seal
I saw only the untidiness of death
Flies stuck to its eyes
Sand up its nose
Feeble flapping of flippers
Bly went back the next day and saw more
He also wished it well in death and did not fight

I felt compelled to "do" something
To "save" the seal
At least to tell a ranger
All I found was a docent
And I didn't like what he said
That they leave nature to its own cycle
Yet he thanked me for my concern

Only now do I realize
That despite how unsatisfactory the response felt to me
I'm learning
Death in nature is what is
We are asked simply to accept

-Ann Muto, 1994

Line one refers to Robert Bly's *"The Dead Seal."*

38

THE ABALONE SONG

Oh, some think that the Lord is fat
And some that He is bony
But as for me, I think that
He is like an abalone.

Oh, some drink rain and some champagne
And whiskey by the pony
But I will try a dash of rye
And a hunk of abalone.

Oh, some like ham and some like jam
And some like macaroni
But our tom-cat lives on fat
And juicy abalone.

I telegraph my better half
By Morse or by Marconi
But when in need of greater speed
I send an abalone.

Oh, Mission Point's a friendly joint
Where every crab's a crony
And true and kind, you'll ever find
The faithful abalone.

He wanders free beside the sea
Wher'er the coast is stony
He flaps his wings and madly sings
The plaintive abalone.

-George Sterling, 1905

39

PELICANS

Four pelicans went over the house,
Sculled their worn oars over the courtyard: I saw that
    ungainliness
Magnifies the idea of strength.
A lifting gale of sea-gulls followed them; slim yachts of the
    element,
Natural growths of the sky, no wonder
Light wings to leave sea; but those grave weights toil, and are
    powerful,
And the wings torn with old storms remember
The cone that the oldest redwood dropped from, the tilting of
    continents,
The dinosaur's day, the lift of new sea-lines.
The omnisecular spirit keeps the old with the new also.
Nothing at all has suffered erasure.
There is life not of our time. He calls ungainly bodies
As beautiful as the grace of horses.
He is weary of nothing; he watches air-planes; he watches
    pelicans.

-Robinson Jeffers, 1925

BIRDS

The fierce musical cries of a couple of sparrowhawks hunting
    on the headland,
Hovering and darting, their heads northwestward,
Prick like silver arrows shot through a curtain the noise of the ocean
Trampling its granite; their red backs gleam
Under my window around the stone corners; nothing gracefuller,
    nothing
Nimbler in the wind. Westward the wave-gleaners,
The old gray sea-going gulls are gathered together,
    the northwest wind wakening
Their wings to the wild spirals of the wind-dance.
Fresh as the air, salt as the foam, play birds in the bright wind,
    fly falcons
Forgetting the oak and the pinewood, come gulls
From the Carmel sands and the sands at the river-mouth, from
    Lobos and out of the limitless
Power of the mass of the sea, for a poem
Needs multitude, multitudes of thoughts, all fierce, all flesh-eaters,
    musically clamorous
Bright hawks that hover and dart headlong, and ungainly
Gray hungers fledged with desire of transgression, salt slimed
    beaks, from the sharp
Rock-shores of the world and the secret waters.

-Robinson Jeffers,1924

OTTERS IN SPRING

The lilac's fragrance filled the air
on a day in the early spring
cloudless the sky made a day fair
and the birds did lustily sing.

At Cypress Grove where the rocks jut up
high above the turbulent ocean
down below a tiny otter pup
fought the water's twirling motion

The ocean tried to suck it in
strong waves washed it towards the rock
and the pup diving tried to swim
under water from this deadly lock

But it really was no match
for the ocean's strength
the mother otter on the watch
came to its rescue at length

On the back with her hands and feet
she paddled through the strong ocean current
making a wake the pup did need
to escape from the deadly torrent.

-Heinz Engler, 1985

POINT LOBOS IN DECEMBER

It was the time when waves house-high
pounded shoals, cliffs, coves
when holdfast could no more defy
waves that broke the fastest holds.

When seaweed, kelp, sargasso beds
were ripped apart and tossed ashore
and nothing there to give fast stead
to our heron who fished there before.

42

We saw the heron on a bough
high up in a dead tree
statue-like he seemed to know
that none him could see.

His gray plumage blended
with the dead tree's branch
only his head extended
as he stood as in trance.

He looked like a tall-coated priest
who gazed across the turbulent ocean
to whom human beings the least
concern for any motion.

Blue-breasted with blue epaulets
and a blue cap on his head
he seemed to be the notion epithet
that the heraldic notion spread.

When plumes atop his long white beak
were lifted by a breeze
a fighting spirit seemed to leap
from eyes that made one freeze.

This picture of silent nobility
came suddenly to an end
when from behind among the trees
I saw a hawk descend.

A short scuffle ensued
a feather floated down
away the heron flew
there cried an angry sound.

His long neck fully extending
his mighty wings slowly moving
the heron for the ocean heading
where no hawk would be intruding.

-*Heinz Engler, 1986*

SEA LION AT GIBSON BEACH

It looked like a hulk of driftwood,
the stubby trunk of a redwood tree
washed ashore on Gibson Beach.
But when we got close,
one end moved, twisted to show
two soft, sea lion eyes.

Contorted, motionless,
it lay, looking at us.
We sat down.
It turned to its stomach,
blotches of sand on its side,
and slowly began to waddle on flippers,
making its ungainly way back to the sea,
casting twisted looks at us, wriggling
like a snake hurrying to shed its skin.
Finally, it reached the ocean,
plunged in, and, with a swiftness too quick to see,
transformed into a sleek, glistening creature,
wet fur aglow in the morning sun,
moving through roiling waters with such ease and grace
that we, beach bound, laughed with joy.

It headed out of the cove towards open water,
the waves singing a chorus of delight,
the kelp waving in welcome,
the water sliding off its body like flute music.

It never looked back.

-Elliot Ruchowitz-Roberts, 1987

RUNNING IN POINT LOBOS

Today I am the massive grey whale,
exploding great bursts of salt spray plumes,
as I glide through roiling seas.

Yesterday I was the fork-antlered, heavy-headed buck
prancing on the needled floor
of moss-drooped pine forests.

Tomorrow...tomorrow
I shall be the wind.
My bare feet will never touch ground.

-Elliot Ruchowitz-Roberts, 1977

A CHRISTMAS WHALE

At Point Lobos,
A primeval
Gnarled finger
Beckoning out over
The Pacific,

In sheet-metal sun
Scattered fog smeared,
In giddy Christmas morning air,
We sat on a knuckle swelled
Granite ridge waiting
For the vanguard whales.

They come across Carmel Bay
Cotton candy plumed knights
In a majestic dance,
In stately Christmas tide,
Caught in our glasses
Rainbow prisms of salt sea
Arced shimmering flat perspective
Fluke flying sea sounding slap.

Once, our granite cliff
Plunged into the ocean
That swelled to it expectant
With the airy intake
Of a surprise gift,
And with it our Christmas whale
That soared white water
Directly below us
Weightless then slowly,
In a geyser of hot animal air,
As a cathedral organ
In a major chord,
Sank from sight
In mighty mystery.

-Don Marsh, 1990

WHALES GOING SOUTH
(Seen from the Big Sur Coast)

Like hilltops turning in a cooler green
As if all earthly springs had lacked the rain
To make up for one always submarine,
Wet bash of flukes, drenched echo in the brain;

For one half-wheel of shoulder half immersed
Not growing flowers now nor any weed
But remnants of Sargassos when they burst
On matted sea-lines curving as they feed.

Humping those arcs, to follow and to flail
Out memories of dry seasons when they stood
Anchored in hill-rows, victims of the fail-
ing waves' estrangement to their seas of blood;

To loss of mile-down deeps and rimless tides
In tropic driftings cooled by their own showers,
Dreamed Tritonward when meadows of their sides
Lay earth-becalmed in seas of grass and flowers!

And now relaunched to plow the hill-change deep,
Led by their bulls in endless moonward runs,
Cruising their seaworn cirque, awake, asleep,
Bulging horizons like a school of suns.

-Eric Barker, 1958

SUNDAY MORNING, POINT LOBOS

Harbor seal pups fan
their forward piebald wings;
females rise to their nuzzling,
bloom interlocking silver rings.
On shore, we quiet
our conversation to witness
the undersea intertwining,
pug-faced pups taking
the feel of floating, diving,
unfolding the riddle of air.
Are you here?
A caterpillar bristled
with tufts of yellow and gray
divines a path in the dust,
an old man's eyebrow gone stray.
Canadian geese nest
in plump touch of succulents,
while a breeze strums the lyre
of a rising blue heron's wings.
A many-faceted eye
draws us all in, distorted
by some understanding
always on the verge of unified.
Are you the most potent
lie we tell ourselves?

-Sarah J. Diehl, 1999

48

CAVE OF THE HEART
North of Granite Point
Vernal Equinox 1991

now I know

why the harbor seals
watched us so closely
why the two hawks

whirled over the wet
woods and wove
through the reeds

why the waves rolled
out of cobalt blue
and leapt white

over black crags
in their crazy rush
for the changing moon

and now to explain

how the gray squalls
processing through the bay
mounted Jacks Peak

while sunrays penetrated
golden interplaying
and spontaneously

doubling hues of
redyellowgreen
indigoviolet

precious little this is

of that light gathered
above the smooth pebbles
shards of shell

of the new sight then given
of the diamonds of the rain
of the egret

of the egret

-John Dotson, 1991

SPRING WALK

Bumblebee in the buckwheat
Lavender seaside daisies
Whorl of orange poppy
Red Indian paintbrush
All on seashore cliffs
Under green pines
Dead branches hung with lichen
Sobbing tide
Restless harbor seals hump themselves
On wet kelp.

-Reda Davis, 2001

50

THE CLIFFS AT ALLAN GROVE

I can't wait to fall asleep tonight
or now even
so I can dream I'm swimming
with the sea lions,
darting through the kelp beds
after fish, hauling
my body out of the sea
onto a warm dry rock to dry myself
yawn
and scratch against its rough beauty

I am impatient to return
to that dreaming state where
I can fly as well as any cormorant,
soar as long as any pelican
stopping only to pluck
a plump juicy fish from the surf
or land on rock islands only they can reach

I must dream
I must know the secrets they know
what is it really like beneath
that stately, graceful,
undulating ceiling of foam
always changing, always the same
how slowly do the kelp forests wave?
where do otters go at night?
what do the other birds really think
of sea gulls?

In a dream I will know.
I can speak their natural tongues
I know the jubilant release of flight
I have the password, the clearance
to roam with los lobos marinos,

to visit bird island, to fly
with two wise old pelicans
and ask them what their kind
knows of love
do they mate for life
and will there ever be another
for me?

-Tom McEntee Jr., 2001

Chapter Five

NOW I KNOW
WHY YOU LOVED STONE

To the Water
Pt. Lobos / S. Smith 02

AT THE TIP OF LOBOS
-for Robinson Jeffers

At the tip of Point Lobos stand the great outcroppings of
     granite: silent, still, light and shadow;
unmoved by the swirling, roiling, foam-covered surf that
     pounds at their base;
unmoved by winds that snap cypress branches; topple pines,
     lift hawk and gull.

Now I know why you loved stone,
why you willed your spirit to lurk in rock:
     the scratch of a dog on the door
     the sword that threatens sons
     the woman's footfalls on the stone stairs.

These granite outcroppings do not weep for the ancient,
     gnarled cypress slowly dying under the fury of the
     wind;
this rock is not moved by the rabbit frozen in fear under the
     shadow of the hawk;
this stone silently bears the cold strokes of the disquiet sea.

Turn your heart to stone. Make stone love stone,
dispassionately, silently, grandly - dark peace -
while the world howls in fury around us.

-Elliot Ruchowitz-Roberts, 1990

REMEMBERING JEFFERS

The lone hawk soars over hills
facing Point Lobos wedding
winged magnificence to clouds
that robe a human majesty--
Robin who walked these cliffs
with sight that flew with hawks
and turned with timeless tides.

Wild surf below sings silvered
stanzas that silver incarnations
close to where his boulders brace
in their weather-beaten tower.

But even stones wear to passing years
there where warnings too wear to a whisper
heard only by a clique of passive poets
shaking heads as rhythmically
as branches of pines and cypress swayed
by Pacific winds, anointed with spray
from the forgiving ocean's peace.

-Lee Richard Hayman, 1981

ROBINSON JEFFERS' CREDO

The beauty of the world for him
was the signature of God
an unsocial bird he had been
cold eyed but with burning blood.

His blood was the water of the sea
that pounded the worn granite drum
he turned away from humanity
to the swell-shaken granite ground.

The tides were in his veins
were wearing his boundaries down
they ate the rock and shifted sands
as he listened to their rocking sound.

He saw the mountains vibrate
from bronze to green year after year
saw dry streams flooded change their shape
saw men changing from joy to fear.

Joy, hope, fear are all in vain
but life and death are not
life is a diamond within
and diamonds outside man must spot.

Life teaches to be faithful in storm
and to be patient of fools
to tolerate many life forms
in face of false prophets stay cool.

In the depth of the ocean
man sees the depth of his soul
where silence and the absence of motion
is the diamond, the hardest coal.

Waves above are lovers of sun
fathers of light, noise, wars, tears, laughter
hot labor, lust, delight and fun
of pain, misery, suffering the mothers.

-Heinz Engler, 1985

ON READING *THE FATE OF THE EARTH*
-for Robinson Jeffers

I hear in rock your silence above roar of surf,
storm wind, gull screech, sea lion yelp.
You watch in craggy featured uninterest.
Should this world blaze through human foolishness,
hot winds scour ocean, crown cypress in flames,
incinerate birds in flight, vaporize the living,
you would continue to watch in stony silence.

Old man,
you are patient; you would sit deep in granite for a million years,
along with ocean and sun and river valley,
and with delight observe in the foaming soup beneath you

new
non-human beginnings.

-Elliot Ruchowitz-Roberts, 1985

CHINA COVE

long boats have landed there
slipping in on water
so clear
it almost isn't there
pirates and buccaneers
wading ashore
to bury treasure
in Robert Louis Stevenson's
imagination

-Ric Masten, 2000

ROBERT BLY AT POINT LOBOS

While I study the red blisters
of lichen on the dying cypress,
he scribbles furiously in the rain,
trying to capture the spirit
of rocks in a smoking sea.

With his clear plastic raincoat
billowing like a fish bladder,
like a bag of waters,
I see him as he truly is—
a stranger, risen among us
from a watery life.

-William Witherup, 1970

THE REGENT OF JANUARY

On the first day of a new year, I sit
      on a stone ledge, use my knees for a desk.
An urgency to capture my impressions
      cascades my words across the page.

Swirling foam & turquoise sea throw
      their laughter against the granite
hem of coast. Revered land, stout backbone,
      repetition of the Santa Lucia Range.

Point Lobos wears her pine & cypress robes,
      her beads of sage & ice plant.
A queen, proud without vanity,
      wise without judgment, alive.

Auburn rust coats stakes that humans place
      to make a civilized path.
Were the gates closed forever, nature
      would soon restore her wild spirit.

Two blues meet on the horizon,
      pastel & sapphire. A breeze carries
the mantra of the restless ocean
      while pelicans glissade above coiling waves.

I close myself in stillness to hear
      the flow of my own current more clearly.
Ebb and progression are but fragments
      of the year's presents.

Perspective expands to include sky
      with earth beneath my feet,
north with south, branch & brine,
      gull whistle, deer mouse & woodmint.

Even in January, new growth shows
  its leaves on skeletons of dried sage.
The back of my hand accepts sunshine
  as my lungs accept wind's bright breath.

In the melding of forested ridge,
  stone-seamed shoals and sleepless tide,
I find the queen's secret.
  When I am gone scatter my words in this sacred place.

-Laura Bayless, 1997

UPON A PAINTER'S DEATH AT CYPRESS GROVE

Cypresses weather-beaten
high above water form a grove
on rocks into the ocean reaching
reaching all souls who there rove.

It was the holy ground of indians
their presence still is felt
with the holy incense
that every river smells.

Painters from far away
feed there on God's wonders
each moment a different portrait
and mood of nature ponders.

There every day the painter's eye
absorbs the many changes
that the weather brought to light
to water, rocks, trees, coastal ranges.

There his eyes had taken
with his last breath a glance
of the spirits that awaken
the soul for its last dance.

-Heinz Engler, 1986

Chapter Six

TO FISH
FOR DEPTH AND MYSTERY

AFTER YEARS
   -to Dick Criley

Desperate for poetry
we had come this far to see Pt. Lobos' peak
in moonlight   its silhouettes
and gleaming waves
on dreaming kayaks, a childhood I might've had
to fish for depth and mystery
among caves like baskets, bowls and openings
tunnels for the long, dark sea.

We'll see the moon rise
above the Highlands before we leave—
promises,
seals, and trees that sough the mainland;
like children still unfinished,
we hoot with soft imaginings
turn our boats
and rock upon the ancient sea.

                    -Matt Friday, 1995

Selection from:
AN ALTAR OF THE WEST
(Point Lobos, the southern boundary of Carmel Bay.)

Beauty, what dost thou here?
Why hauntest thou this empery of pain
Where men in vain
Long for another sphere?
Art not an exile shy,
A dreamer 'mid the swords,
Upon this iron world where men defy
Time and its hidden lords?
Thou waitest with a splendor on thy brow,
And seem'st to watch with compensating eyes
Each jest our dwarfing Fates devise;
And after all the strife,
'Tis thou
Who standest where the slayers' feet have trod -
Perchance a portion of this dream of God
That will not go from life....

And yet we sigh,
Who find on land and sea thy radiant touch
And dream thou hast on earth a secret nook -
A glade supremely blest
In woodlands where thou wanderest unseen.
Hath not the snowy North
Or star-concealing ocean of the West
A court wherein thou sittest queen,
A temple whence thou goest forth,
An altar for our quest?
Goddess, one such I know,
And fain would praise,
Tho less the gift my words bestow
Than tapers 'mid the blaze
Of peaceless stars that gather at thy throne.
Yet seems it most thine own.

Past Carmel lies a headland that the deep -
A Titan at his toil -
Has graven with the measured surge and sweep

Of waves that broke ten thousand years ago.
Here winds assoil
That blow
From unfamiliar skies
And isolating water of the West.
Deep-channelled by the billows' rage it lies,
As tho the land
Thrust forth a vast, tree-shaggy hand
To bar the furious ocean from its breast.
Here Beauty would I seek,
For this I deem her home,
And surely here
The sea-adoring Greek,
Poseidon, unto thee
Thy loftiest temple had been swift to rear,
Of chosen marble and chalcedony,
Pure as the irrecoverable foam....

-George Sterling, 1911

It is possible my friend
If I have had a fat belly
That the wolf lives on fat
Gnawing slowly
Through a visceral night of rancor.
It is possible that the absence of pain
May be so great
That the possibility of care
May be impossible.

Perhaps to know pain.
Anxiety, rather than the fear
Of the fear of anxiety.
This talk of miracles!

Of Animism:
I have been in a spot so full of spirits
That even the most joyful animist
Brooded
When all in sight was less to be cared about
Than death
And there was no noise in the ears
That mattered.
(I knelt in the shade
By a cold salt pool
And felt the entrance of hate
On many legs,
The soul like a clambering
Water vascular system.

No scuttling could matter
Yet I formed in my mind
The most beautiful
Of maxims.
How could I care

For your illness or mine?)
This talk of bodies!

It is impossible to speak
Of lupine or tulips
When one may read
His name
Spelled by the mold on the stumps
When the forest moves about one.

Heel. Nostril.
Light. Light! Light!
This is the bird's song
You may tell it
to your children.

-Michael McClure, 1955

CENTRAL COAST OLIVE-BRANCH
PT. LOBOS CYPRESS/S. SMITH/02

SHOE CHASER AT POINT LOBOS

First reports claimed it was a four year old girl,
Later that it was a five year old boy, which as
It turned out, was true, fresh from Kansas wheat
Seas with his vacationing family, his toes tasting
Pacific sand for the very first time. He posed
Boldly for his father's Pentax, then in fractured
Time, he turned to give chase, April's ocean having
Reached out for his small shoes which he had left
On a granite shoulder on Monastery Beach. He raced
After them and April's ocean stole him too,
Christening him gone.
What I did not tell you about that day was that
I stayed there for several hours, watching the
Father stalk the golden crescent well into night
Long after the helicopter and divers had gone
Home. This father from Kansas, scouring sea's edge
For his forever gone wheat sailor.
I watched from my perch on the century-old
Eucalyptus root, a screaming whisper raging down
Through the hard bones of my inner ear, a voice
Promising me that you would leave me someday,
Give up on us and soar away, rising so quickly
Above my killing carelessness that I could run
Bare toed across every ocean for all time
And never find you.

-Allston James, 2002

LACE LICHEN & DEAD TREES
PT. LOBOS / S. SMITH·02

72

MONASTERY BEACH

Blinking eyelid slice of sand,
Alluring, timeless rocky bend,
Rendezvous of faith and fate,
Innocents and renegades.

Shore of fatal interludes,
Unsought death, Pacific blues,
Tourists, divers, anglers, bums,
Close calls, chapel, praying nuns.

White steeple adorned by cross
Hews to myth fraught ancient loss.
Beach below it sandy, bare;
Unread signs - no cross to dare.

Off the rocks or off the sand,
Ocean's foam-clad iron hand
Downward tugs and seaward yanks
Hapless, thrashing mendicants.

Forty-four by local count,
Untowardly outward bound.
(Fogbow, moon, San Jose Creek,
Witness fateful hide and seek)

Freed of mundane surface vows,
Swept along by undertows,
Ultimately safe from self,
Past the kelp and past the shelf.

Weaning amniotic float,
Ephemeral one-way tote,
Plasma of eternal lust
Contravening "dust to dust."

-William Gluck, 1991

NORTH SHORE TRAIL

On any trail,
There is always someone
Ahead or behind.

Already we had come
Face to face
With two deer.
There was no trace
Of fear in their eyes.

Now, two people
Were coming toward us.
A woman, and a young man
We learned was her son.
The woman, out of breath,
Told us she had emphysema.
But it surprised her,
How well she could walk
Along the trails.
It's the air, we decided.
And the peace, she said.
I have my trusty inhaler,
She said, patting her pocket.
But her smile told us
She would not need it.

We went our separate ways
On the trail that led us all
Deeper into the shrine
Of magic, and healing.

-Christopher Woods, 2001

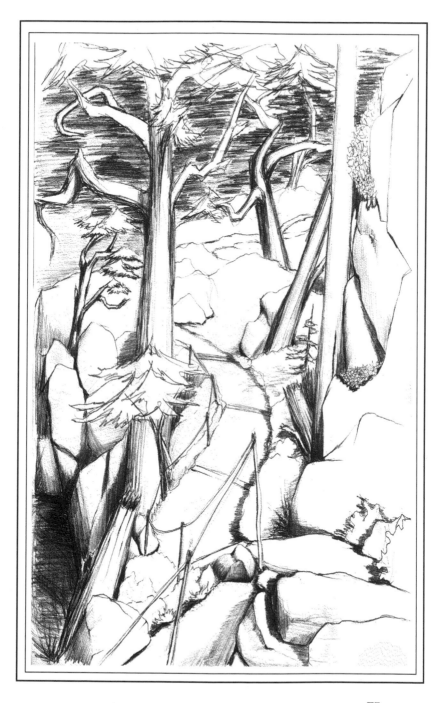

THERE IS NO LEGEND OF THIS PLACE

There is no legend of this place
no myth of Gods or men
that being told could be translated
into our tongue,
or being translated could be understood
of our mind.
This is a lost place - out of the memory of the race -
of any known race.
One goes into it unaware;
one comes out from it haunted
as the trees are haunted
and the undying rocks
and the dark groves where fear is.
These that are here have no likeness;
they are not troubled as we are troubled;
they move on different feet - they look with other eyes
on a sea that holds their ships -
ships that come and go,
mysterious as thought -
shadows in a moon.

-*Jeanne D'Orge, 1928*

IF I COULD NOT SHUT MY EYES

If I could not shut my eyes -
if I could not close my mind
sharply - like a door against it
how would I dare to climb this burning height -
look down and let it all come in at once...
I should die;
rocks would shatter me;
the passionate trees crash down;
and the sea - the sea would spring up in all its beauty
even to this great height.
Or I should leap down to it
so to be finished with the ecstacy -
so to lie forever
like an empty shell
with only soft blue water flowing through
and unheard song.

-Jeanne D'Orge, 1928

POINT LOBOS

This is a place to remember and renew,
Here is the genesis of my Being;
              I confess sins
To the wildflowers, and receive forgiveness
              In the brown eyes of deer,
And the angels of the Lord
              Are the guardian stags,
And I am a keeper of Eden.
              To love the living wood
As flesh, and running water
              As any human speech
Is not unnatural, but a returning,
              Here things fall
From flux forever, and change mouths
              The whitened knuckles of the stone.
Protected from jackals,
Who bundle and burn the orchards for suburbs,
The cypress rest in their long retreat,
              They climb the sea cliffs
Over Devil's Cauldron,
              Where above a storm
The wintering whales
Trail south to mate, moving slowly to sea
              With mysteries to be born.

-Kirk Hall, 1978

SYMPHONY GRAND

You lovers of music, come listen to me;
To you I would speak of a Symphony Grand.

The instruments played, with consummate skill,
Are the Sun, and the Sky with the Clouds scudding by;
The Wind, and the Sea with its blanket of Fog;
The Trees, and the Birds with their delicate Songs;
The Flowers and Shrubs, all in color profuse;
The Animals on land, and those in the Sea.

Oh, come with me now to a place called Point Lobos.
Oh, come and be thrilled, by the sounds not alone,
For each sense you possess, haunting rhythms abound,
And harmonies fulfill the desires of your Soul.
Anytime we may go, for the concert never ceases.
And oft we must go, for the concert ever changes.

-David Covell, 1996

PT. LOBOS

It's the grandest meeting of land and sea
A place where poet and painter long to be
It's more that deer in the meadow and a sea lion's bark
For Pt. Lobos isn't just a park

Pt. Lobos isn't just a park, it's a feeling
With sights and sounds and smells to all senses appealing
With sailor, priest and scholar part of its history
Many a morning fog shrouds it with mystery

The mighty waves batter her shore
Yet the sturdy coast comes back for more
Much like the human spirit standing against every foe
With each new test a chance to grow

Yes, Pt. Lobos is more than just a sight
It's somewhere to be to make all things right
Pt. Lobos is more than just a place
Pt. Lobos is a smile on God's face

-Roy Coon, 1991

Map
&
Notes on Contributors

INDEX
TO THE LOCATIONS
OF POEMS & DRAWINGS

(can you find them all?)

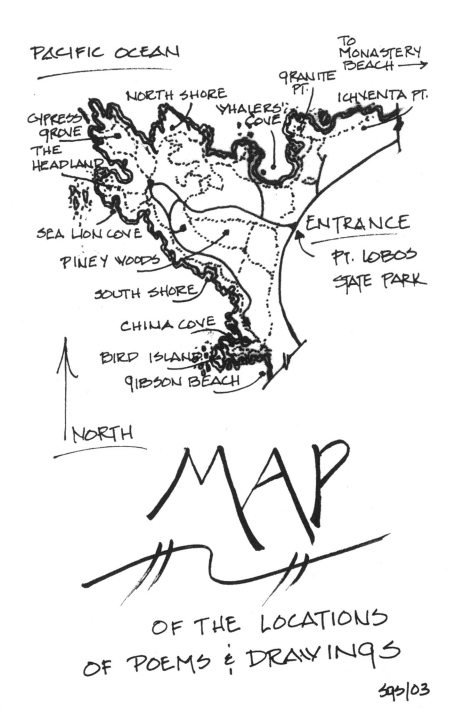

PACIFIC OCEAN

TO MONASTERY BEACH →

GRANITE PT.

ICHXENTA PT.

NORTH SHORE

WHALERS' COVE

CYPRESS GROVE

THE HEADLAND

ENTRANCE

PT. LOBOS STATE PARK

SEA LION COVE

PINEY WOODS

SOUTH SHORE

CHINA COVE

BIRD ISLAND

GIBSON BEACH

NORTH

MAP

OF THE LOCATIONS
OF POEMS & DRAWINGS

sgs/03

83

Contributors

The Editor:

Deborah Streeter is a docent at Point Lobos. A minister in the United Church of Christ since 1983, she has been a parish minister, campus minister and hospital chaplain. She moved to Palo Colorado Canyon near Big Sur in 1996 and started a new ministry called Upwellings: a Ministry of Environmental Stewardship. She is also a guide at the Monterey Bay Aquarium, and serves on the Monterey Bay National Marine Sanctuary Advisory Council and the Point Lobos Natural History Association Board.

The Artist:

Sally Smith grew up in Orono, Maine. She studied art at Wellesley College and at the University of Maine. Her teacher Vincent Hartgen, with Frank Hamabe, helped inspire a generation of artists to build on the work of Winslow Homer, John Marin, William Zorach, and Fairfield and Eliot Porter, who all lived - at least in the summers!- in Maine. This tradition has inspired her and the art and photography on California's Central Coast. She has a studio in Carmel and is part of the California State University at Monterey Bay community.

The Poets:

Eric Barker (1905-1973), a native of England, lived as a "poet and gardener" in Big Sur from 1953 until his death. He published six books of poetry, and his poems appeared in many respected journals, such as *Saturday Review, Yale Review, Harper's* and *The Atlantic Monthly*. He received four prestigious awards, including the Shelley Memorial Award in 1962. "Point Lobos Cy-

84

presses" is from his *Directions in the Sun,* 1956 and "Whales Going South" is from *A Ring of Willows,* 1962.

Laura Bayless, a Carmel native, is the author of *White Stream and Touchstones,* in which "The Regent of January" and "Enough Words" first appeared, and *The Edge of the Nest* .

Robert Bly, is an acclaimed poet, essayist, translator and social activist. Winner of the National Book Award for his poetry, he has also brought many foreign poets to U.S. attention through his translations. He has done much to promote men's consciousness, through writings and workshops. For years he has brought creative writing classes to Point Lobos. (See William Witherup's poem, p. 60.) "Some Rocks Off Point Lobos Near China Cove" has not appeared before in print.

Roy Coon, retired high school teacher and author of *Tuesday Morning,* has been a Point Lobos docent since 1985. "Pt. Lobos" first appeared in the *Point Lobos Natural History Association Newsletter.*

David Covell, retired scientist, is a long-term Point Lobos docent. "Symphony Grand" was first published in the *Point Lobos Natural History Association Newsletter.*

Curt Cureton, State Parks aide and Point Lobos docent, is a retired teacher. "Veteran Cypress" first appeared in the *Point Lobos Natural History Association Newsletter.*

Reda Davis frequently took the bus to Point Lobos from her Pacific Grove home to paint. She died in 2002 and bequeathed the bulk of her estate, from the sale of two houses, to the Point Lobos Natural History Association. Before her death, she wrote the following biography for this book: "I'm a member of the Pacific Grove Heritage

Society to promote historic preservation. Let us not become a chip on the edge of Silicon Valley." "Spring Walk" is published here for the first time.

Lucille Lang Day is the author of four poetry collections, including *Infinities*, in which "At Point Lobos" first appeared. She is the founder and director of Scarlet Tanager Books and director of the Hall of Health Museum in Berkeley.

Sarah Diehl has hiked at Point Lobos for 30 years. She is on the staff of the Center for Nonproliferation Studies at the Monterey Institute of International Studies and author of the reference book, *Nuclear Weapons and Non-proliferation*. Her poems have been published in local journals.

Jeanne D'Orge (1877-1964) was a poet and artist in the circle of William Carlos Williams, Marianne Moore and Wallace Stevens in New York. She and her second husband Carl Cherry were active in the Carmel arts scene in the 30's and 40's. D'Orge founded the Carl Cherry Center in his honor in 1948, now known for its collection of D'Orge writings and paintings, as wells as lectures, concerts, poetry readings, art exhibits and theater productions. Her poems in this book are all from her chapbook *Point Lobos*, 1928, reprinted by the Carl Cherry Center in 2003.

John Dotson, a Monterey area author, artist and educator, was the first poet in residence at the Robinson Jeffers Tor House Foundation. The poems in this book first appeared in the *Point Lobos Natural History Association Newsletter*.

Heinz Engler (1920-98), left his native Germany after W.W.II and followed Route 66 and his beloved *Grapes of*

86

Wrath to settle on the Monterey Peninsula. He served as Chairman of the German Department at the Defense Language Institute in Monterey. His regular visits to Point Lobos inspired over 100 poems, which are in a volume at the Point Lobos Docent Library. His poems here were also published in the *Point Lobos Natural History Association Newsletter*. "Upon a Painter's Death at Cypress Grove" refers to a time when Engler's daughter Renata used CPR on a painter, Conrad Schwiering, at Point Lobos in an effort to revive him.

Matt Friday is a widely published poet. He edited a Monterey Bay area anthology, *Small Towns, Roadstops, and Cafes*, 1993, and co-founded the Gay Lesbian Bisexual Transgender newspaper *The Paper* in 1994. He is an editor at CTB/McGraw-Hill. "After Years" first appeared in the *Point Lobos Natural History Association Newsletter*. Dick Criley, to whom the poem is dedicated, worked with Matt on the board of the local ACLU chapter, and lived next door to Point Lobos all his life.

William Gluck, a native of Hungary, learned English at age 26. A retired engineer and inventor, he is a founding member of the Humanist Association of the Monterey Bay Area.

Jean Grace teaches Earth Sciences (Geography and Geology) at Monterey Peninsula College. She was twice elected as Mayor of Carmel, 1988-92. She has served as President of the Asilomar Corporation for State Parks, and on the boards of the Robinson Jeffers Tor House Foundation and the Big Sur Land Trust. "March Equinox 1996" first appeared in the *Point Lobos Natural History Association Newsletter*.

Dora Hagemeyer (1891-1989), a native of Australia, grew up in New Zealand, and moved to Carmel in 1923. She wrote more than twenty small volumes of poetry, was an accomplished watercolorist, and was a leader in the Carmel arts community until her death. "Cliff Cypresses" is from her *White Sands of Carmel*, 1947, and "Cypress Trees at Point Lobos" is from *The Quicken Tree*, 1953.

Kirk Hall divides his time between the Central Coast and Mariposa, near Yosemite. He has written two books of poetry, *Angel of the Cities* and *Whispers of an Inward Dream*, in which "Point Lobos" first appeared.

Lee Richard Hayman has taught poetry in high schools and university. A published poet, he has served on the Robinson Jeffers Tor House Foundation. "Remembering Jeffers" was first published in the journal *Ally* in 1982.

Ed Huenerfauth visited Point Lobos every year for 35 years from his native Chicago, after seeing Edward Weston's photographs. Upon retirement he moved to the area in 1998 and pursued his own photographic interests.

Allston James teaches English and Literature at Monterey Peninsula College. He has written two poetry chapbooks, *The Mile Away Contessa* and *Paris Beach*, in which "Shoe Chaser at Point Lobos" first appeared.

Robinson Jeffers (1887-1962) moved to Carmel in 1913 and in 1918 began building his signature Tor House from local granite boulders. From this rugged windswept home he could look across Carmel Bay to Point Lobos. Jeffers wrote long narratives of "this coast crying out for tragedy," shorter meditative lyrics like those in this collection, and dramas on classical themes, including the critically acclaimed adaptation of *Medea*. Jeffers said of his landscape and poetry: "My love, my loved subject:

mountain and ocean, rock, water and beasts and trees/
Are the protagonists; the human people are only sym-
bolic interpreters." Jeffers wrote almost 30 volumes of
poetry. His complete writings have recently been pub-
lished by Stanford University Press. Tor House is regu-
larly open for tours: www.torhouse.org

Josh Jossi (1948-1997) lived and wrote poetry on the
Monterey Peninsula for over 20 years. For two summers
he led poetry walks in Yosemite National Park. This
poem first appeared in his book, *Back to the Source*, 1986.

Dustin Katz lives in the San Francisco Bay Area. He is
currently 12 years old. His interests include swimming,
biking, Legos and playing computer games. This is his
first published poem.

Don Marsh (1928-2002) was a published novelist and
poet. He wrote about where he lived, for the first half of
his life, New York City; the second half, Carmel.

Ric Masten, a Big Sur poet, artist, and songwriter, has
toured extensively for 35 years, performing his "talking
poetry" at more than 400 colleges and universities. He is
the author of 16 books, including *Let It Be A Dance: Words
and One-Liners*. A man of many talents, he is a Unitarian-
Universalist minister, builder and printer. "China Cove"
first appeared in *Pacific Light: Images of the Monterey
Peninsula*, 2002.

Michael McClure was a founding member of the Beat
Generation. In 1959, at age 22, he read "Point Lobos:
Animism" at his first poetry reading, the historic Six
Gallery reading in San Francisco, at which Allen
Ginsburg first read his poem "Howl." He has produced
16 books of poetry, six collections of essays, two novels,
and ten plays, including the Obie-winning *Josephine the*

Mouse Singer and the notorious *The Beard*. He is also co-writer, with Janis Joplin, of the song "Mercedes Benz," and professor at California College of Arts and Crafts.

Tom McEntee Jr. is a public library professional by day and a writer by night. A San Francisco native, he has a B.A. in creative writing from S.F. State and he is active in the Swedenborgian Church of San Francisco. "The Cliffs at Allan Grove" is his first published poem.

Ann Muto was born in a War Relocation Authority Camp in Arizona during W.W. II. A graduate of UC Berkeley and San Jose State, she worked in pubic education as a teacher and administrator. Now retired, she enjoys writing and traveling, especially to Point Lobos.

Elliot Ruchowitz-Roberts has lived across from Point Lobos for 35 years. He is co-author of *Bowing to Receive the Mountain: Essays by Lin Jensen and Poems by Elliot Roberts*; co-editor/co-translator of two works from Telugu; and co-editor of a college text. He serves on the Boards of the Robinson Jeffers Tor House Foundation, the Henry Miller Memorial Library and the Monterey Chapter of the ACLU. The poems in this collection were first published in the *Point Lobos Natural History Association Newsletter*.

Clinton Scollard (1860-1932) taught English at Hamilton College, 1887-1898 and then devoted his life to writing. He was a very popular and widely published poet. "Lyrics of Lobos" appeared in *An Anthology of Verse*, published in 1925 by the San Francisco Writers Club.

George Sterling (1869-1926), was a central figure in Carmel's Bohemian art scene from 1905, when he moved there, until his death. Friends with Ambrose Bierce, Jack London, and Mary Austin, Sterling organized many a

90

drunken picnic at Point Lobos, at which the famous "Abalone Song" was composed. He helped scatter the ashes of his beloved fellow poet Nora May French at Point Lobos in 1907. Author of eleven volumes of poetry and four verse dramas, Sterling wrote a critical work on Robinson Jeffers and a number of short stories. Beat poet and publisher Lawrence Ferlinghetti has described Sterling as "a kind of leashed Swinburne." The selection from "Altar of the West" is from a much longer poem found in *The House of Orchids and Other Poems*, 1911.

Illia Thompson teaches Creative Writing and Journaling in the Carmel area. She is nationally published, and has written *Heartframes*, a collection of poems. "New Year's Day" was first published in the *Monterey County Herald*.

William Witherup lived in Big Sur in the 1970's. He is the author of eight books of poetry, the most recent being *Down Wind, Down River: New and Selected Poems*, (West End Press, 2000) in which "Robert Bly at Point Lobos" first appeared. He currently lives in Seattle and is active in prison reform.

Christopher Woods is the author of a novel, a prose collection and a stage monologue collection. He lives in Houston with his wife. They make an annual pilgrimage to Point Lobos.